The Hearts of the Fathers

BJ Emerson

with Allen M. Emerson, Jr.

Behold, I will send you Elijah the prophet
before the coming of the great and dreadful day
of the LORD. And he will turn the hearts of the
fathers to the children, and the hearts of the
children to their fathers, lest I come and strike
the earth with a curse.

Malachi 4:5–6 NKJV

The events and conversations in this book have been set down to the best of the author's ability, although some names and details have been changed to protect the privacy of individuals.

Unless otherwise noted, all scripture is taken from the New Revised Standard Version Bible, copyright © 1989 the Division of Christian Education of the National Council of the Churches of Christ in the United States of America. Used by permission. All rights reserved.

Scripture marked NKJV is taken from the New King James Version®. Copyright © 1982 by Thomas Nelson. Used by permission. All rights reserved.

Published by Buzzadelic, LLC | Greenville NC
First paperback edition January 2020

Book design by BJ Emerson

ISBN 978-0-578-60749-8

Acknowledgements

To the many volunteers and chaplains who ministered to my father in prison, we thank you. We hope this story encourages your hearts and confirms your calling in the ministry of reconciliation.

For those on the other side of our family tree who labored for years in prayer, we thank you. The impact of those prayers is evident throughout the pages of this book, and the effects will touch many.

We acknowledge God, who orchestrated this remarkable story of hope and restoration; Jesus, who gives us access to the Father; and the Holy Spirit, who draws us all.

The Hearts of the Fathers

Introduction

The year was 2004. The three of us stood holding hands in a small circle on the gravel driveway. The Florida trailer park was so far from where it all started some 40 years before. Like most stories, ours goes back even further, but the best place to start is around the time my grandfather disappeared.

We prayed as I held hands with the most unlikely of men. In one hand, the best man at my second wedding: my ex-convict father. In the other, a Navy deserter and retired trucker who had run for many miles until life finally caught up with him. The two of them had been miraculously reunited just a year earlier.

Regrettably, this would be the only meeting I would have with my grandfather.

How this driveway prayer meeting came to be could not have been scripted. I do not remember the prayer specifically, but this reunion represented something remarkable—the resolution of a story that would shake a family tree and touch countless lives. Certainly mine. And now yours.

Chapter 1

WREAKING HAVOC

Scrolling through the newspaper archives, I am reminded of the hopeless conditions we faced in the summer of 1984. Among others, headlines included "Man suspected in hoax charged in Pennsylvania," "Jail term set in extortion," and "Prison term is begun by 'bomber.'" I had not bothered with many of the details at the time, or perhaps my mother shielded my brother and me from them as the Associated Press story was featured in papers all over the East Coast. Apparently 26 counts of extortion and bomb threats across three states is big news. My father's addictions to drugs, alcohol, and gambling drove him to find creative and bold ways to get money to support his lifestyle—a lifestyle I observed from a distance as a young teenager. I knew about the drugs he sold out of the mini-mart he managed and the former nightclub dancer he lived with; it was the other more newsworthy pastimes that somehow escaped me.

After planting authentic-looking bombs in a restaurant or supermarket, typically in the bathroom, my father would then call the business threatening to remotely detonate the fake device if demands for cash were not met. It worked around half the time, and this continued throughout much of 1983. The spree came to an end, however, when a concerned passerby turned in his license plate number during one such transaction.

When officials, including the FBI, raided his home on May 4, 1984, they found the evidence they needed, and Allen Michael Emerson, Jr. was placed under arrest.

"He was wreaking havoc everywhere," according to Assistant D.A. Robert Adshead, as reported in *The Philadelphia Inquirer*. "He was having buildings evacuated on a regular basis."

Between federal and state time, we calculated he could be facing up to 76 years behind bars. We would later learn that "copycat" criminals would try to reproduce the relative success of his crimes.

Needless to say, "role model" was not a term one would use when talking about my father. Divorced from my mother before I can remember, he was largely absent as my older brother and I were growing up. Now it looked like more than distance would separate us, possibly for good. When I was 14 years old, my father headed off to a federal prison in Springfield, Missouri.

Bomb threats and FBI aside, 1984 was interesting for many reasons. Apple introduced the Macintosh computer, Gandhi was assassinated, and Michael Jackson released "Thriller." Like most teenagers, my life was fully immersed in things like MTV, a heavy metal band where I played bass guitar, and a giant pentagram tapestry I hung on my bedroom wall. My brother had gone off to college, and a remarriage for my mother left me exploring new levels of independence in all kinds of directions, none of which had any promise or purpose.

Chapter 2

ABSENT WITHOUT LEAVE

A generation before, my grandfather had left in a different way. Allen Emerson, Sr. seemed to vanish from the family picture shortly after my father was born. For many years, we had no idea if he was even alive. All we knew was he had joined the U.S. Navy near the end of World War II. In 1995, I submitted a request to the Department of Defense to release his military personnel records, this was something that was supposedly allowed only if the service member was deceased. While we could not confirm it, I suspect the person reviewing my request took one look at his extensive disciplinary record and promptly put a copy in the mail after assuming he was dead.

It quickly became evident from his records that desertion and being Absent Without Leave (AWOL) had become a habit for my grandfather. I was interested to find that he had the same job rating I did when I served in the Navy a few wars later. What we did not have in common was the brig time and bad conduct discharge. In the context of the war, and only having finished school through the ninth grade, I suppose his service is something to be honored. His service ended with one last unauthorized absence. After being gone more than four months, he surrendered himself just three days after my father was born.

He served a seven-month sentence and returned to his family in New Hampshire late in 1948. Shortly thereafter, the couple parted ways and left my father to be raised by his grandmother. My father remembers a brief visit at the age of 10 when his father came through town driving a Red Ball moving truck. Then nothing.

My grandfather, Allen Sr., with my grandmother, Kathleen Geraci

Another mystery exists with Allen Sr.'s parents. Unmarried when she had my grandfather in the late '20s, it seems my great-grandmother had no choice but to stick with her maiden name of Emerson. Interestingly enough, we can trace the family line back to colonial America and a revolutionary who fought for Massachusetts.

There is no record of my great-grandfather. In fact, the "Father" entry on my grandfather's birth certificate is blank.

As a young man, you are supposed to be able to look up at the family tree and find inspiration, not incarceration—legacy, not felony. There were, however, many godly people on the other side of my family tree, and I suspect their prayers had an impact on the brokenness of my paternal side.

My grandfather was nowhere to be found, and my father was facing the possibility of prison for the rest of his life. The thread of abandonment in the men on that side of my family was clear. The term "generational curse" comes to mind, and there did not seem to be an end to it.

I remember wondering how one would go about cutting down his family tree. With little hope, my own trajectory and destiny were questionable at best.

The Hearts of the Fathers

Chapter 3

LAYERS OF BITTERNESS

For my father, parenthood had been limited to infrequent and sporadic summer vacations or stays at his converted garage apartment in Vermont. When it came time for a visit, my brother and I were always anxiously waiting when he came to pick us up. Maybe we were just restless kids, but it seemed he was always hours or days late. Trips were filled with fishing stories, go-cart tracks, and camping adventures. They were always fun but rarely meaningful. My brother and I were quite a handful being just 13 months apart in age. Keeping the two of us unruly kids entertained was not something for which my father was equipped.

We could take a simple visit to the laundromat and make it exciting. Racing through the building in laundry carts worked for a while, but when my father told us about the time he went around inside a dryer, we had to give it a go as well. As it turns out, a short person can wedge themselves in a commercial dryer while someone holds the door open and presses down the button. To keep cool, we put in some damp clothes. That was the summer I managed to go around in a dryer 169 times. I had to beat my dad's record after all.

One Christmas, just before his incarceration, my father arrived with a large gift wrapped box in the back seat. We ran out to his car and tore off the paper to discover nothing but a note inside. The note said something about being robbed and not having any money for gifts but held a promise of new snow skis. As I recall, we went shopping for them some weeks later.

Like I think any young boy wants to be, I was always proud of my dad but for a variety of reasons at any given time. Early on I bragged about him being a crazy, irresponsible bad-ass—until he went to prison, of course, but even that information could be leveraged at the right time if needed. Making that part of your reputation in high school could serve to be helpful in the event there was trouble.

My father's incarceration, however, would cause him to miss a number of critical events throughout those teenage years. Fathers are supposed to be there when you get your license and your first car or graduate from high school and boot camp. You are supposed to see him in the audience and hear his encouragement

19

and support from the stands. Additionally, I managed to cram a wedding and the birth of my first child into the long list of critical events that happened during the time he was gone.

A prison visit in 1987 with my dad (center) and brother Scott (right)

But even if there were cheers, I could not hear them coming from his prison cell. I would get letters and we would talk on the phone, but time after time, the uncertainty of a release date meant another missed event. And with each one, another layer of bitterness would be added to the growing pile of disillusionment and disappointment.

The calls and visits became more infrequent as I went off into the military at age 18 in search of something to satisfy the restless void now firmly set in my own heart.

The Hearts of the Fathers

Chapter 4

DIVINE CONSPIRATORS

Once occupied by inmates Larry Flynt and John Gotti, the federal prison in Springfield, Missouri, was the first stop for my father. The events and cast of characters assembled for the two months my father would spend there were divinely orchestrated from day one to be a real heart transplant.

On August 6, 1984, he looked around the receiving and discharge area, where a fellow inmate gave him the good news.

"No one has escaped from here since 1938."

Once inside, the news shifted toward an even more eternal narrative. It began with the little Hawaiian guy in for embezzlement who simply let my father know, "You need Jesus."

Other inmates started inviting him to the chapel services held by volunteers from a local Assemblies of God church with students from two nearby Christian colleges.

One of the prison nurses he interacted with on a regular basis was another divine conspirator. She was prohibited, however, from interacting around the area of faith but regularly let my father know she was praying for him. Every day he walked up and down the stairs on the block, and there she was. Her covert seed-planting did not go unnoticed by my father, and she served as a daily reminder of the apparent interest God had in his life.

At one point during that time, he was sitting in his cell on top of a heater and looked down to see an open Bible. Highlighted on the pages below was the very first verse he had ever read.

Call to Me, and I will answer you, and show you great and mighty things, which you do not know.

Jeremiah 33:3 NKJV

His response was "Yeah, right." While directly challenging my father's pride and know-it-all attitude, this book was also presenting an invitation—one that was growing more attractive each day given the situation in which my father found himself.

As the others persisted with offers to attend chapel services, my father finally agreed to attend, but he was not the kind of guy who wanted a hug from a volunteer and he told them so.

"If anyone tries to hug me, I'll knock them the #$&% out."

I suspect that the education those young, innocent college student ministers were getting was priceless. But through it all, my father started to learn just how much God truly loved him.

Something changed a couple weeks later. On Thursday, August 23, he walked down the stairs with an altogether different countenance.

Seeing his face, the nurse could not help herself when she shouted, "You've been born again!" only to quickly cover her mouth with her hand.

"Yes, yes, I guess I have," my father replied.

It was in that federal prison cell in Springfield, Missouri, that my father made a single decision that would impact generations. This decision was based on Joshua's declaration in Joshua 24:15.

"But as for me and my household, we will serve the LORD."

My father started trusting God with his life, but there were other people he cared about. With good reason, two of his biggest concerns were my brother and me. During phone calls with my mother, she would tell him about the trouble we were getting into, and he was all too familiar with the direction we were heading in.

Another concern was for his father, although he did not even know if he was dead or alive. He had not heard from him in over 30 years. Regardless, he started praying, and in his reading of the Bible, he ran across this promise.

The Lord will perfect that which concerns me.

Psalm 138:8 NKJV

His prayer for all of us was simple. "God, please send someone to share the gospel with them."

My father wanted us to experience the same love and forgiveness that he had come to know through Jesus Christ.

It was through these bold prayers that a chain reaction began in my family tree. These prayers would certainly be answered, although in ways that could never be imagined.

Chapter 5

UNSHAKEN

Much of my father's time in prison the first year was spent going back and forth between federal facilities and Pennsylvania county jails. With a few weeks here and a few days there, the bulk of his time was spent in Danbury, Connecticut.

In Danbury, 140 inmates shared each dorm, with individual "cubes" or cells. My father's cell was different in that it was smaller in size and featured a steam pipe running along the ceiling and over the desk. When the pipe became a regular complaint after numerous head bumps, an observer across the hall challenged my father about the situation.

"Why don't you do what the Bible says about that?"

Give thanks in all circumstances; for this is the will of God in Christ Jesus for you.

1 Thessalonians 5:18

Giving thanks for the "stupid steam pipe," as it came to be called, made no sense. Initially with a sour attitude and feelings of hypocrisy, my father started to do what the Bible said and started giving thanks. After a couple days, his attitude began to change, and he chose to be content with it.

It was 1986, and riots in a Lorton, Virginia, facility had forced the transfer of over 600 inmates to other facilities, including Danbury. Along with them came bunk beds in each cube, effectively doubling occupation—

with the exception of the cubes with the steam pipes running through them because the beds would not fit. My father's cube remained a single room when everyone else had to double up. Giving thanks all of a sudden made a whole lot of sense, and others took note of his relatively lavish accommodations.

One inmate doing time for mafia-related activities approached my father with a proposition related to his now upgraded residence. "Does your family need anything back home?"

Apparently, he had connections on the outside and was prepared to make a trade. My father declined the offer, understanding that God had a hand in putting him there and had taught him a very important lesson about being thankful in all circumstances.

Passing through a Michigan prison at one point, a poem that had been scribbled on the underside of the bunk above where he slept caught his eye.

"Two men in prison,
looking through the bars.
One sees the mud,
the other sees the stars."

A version of the 1896 Frederick Langbridge poem, these two very different perspectives among inmates were becoming clear to my father. He could tell who was focused on those things above or below, and they seemed to have different outcomes as a result.

The boldness my father had, which helped land him in prison, was not lost once he became a believer. One day, he was among a large group of inmates rushing out to the prison yard after lunch when a big Latino ran into my father. The drama of some bad drug deal had this character rather upset as the busy crowd surrounded them.

My father was clear regarding his need when he fearlessly told him, "Man, you need Jesus in your life."

"Don't tell me what I need in my life or I'll kill ya," was the reply.

Unshaken, my father ended the conversation with, "You got the devil in you, and I have Jesus in me. You're not going to do anything."

Frustrated and confused, the man went on his way.

Six weeks later my father was being transferred to the State Correctional Institution in Cresson, Pennsylvania. Shackled in the bus seat next to him for the long trip was none other than the angry Latino.

"I remember you," was all the Latino said, and for the next eight hours, my father shared Christ with him, even while he pretended to sleep.

Every jail and prison brought different challenges and experiences, often with demonstrations of the power and grace of God. At times, God's presence was so tangible it would impact others. At one prison, my father was sleeping in a two-man cell when his bed started shaking—not in a bad way but in an Acts chapter 4 kind of way.

When they had prayed, the place in which they were gathered together was shaken; and they were all filled with the Holy Spirit and spoke the word of God with boldness.

Acts 4:31

My father shared the cell with a man named Jim, and after being awakened the first time by the violent bed-shaking he looked around and checked with Jim to see if it was all just in his head. Jim had not seen anything, so they tried to go back to sleep. Within minutes, my father's bed-shaking picked up where it had left off, this time moving the bed toward the center of the room. Jim was coherent enough to witness this, so they both got up and tried to figure out what was going on, without success. All they knew was that they had experienced the power of a living God who had gripped them in a way they could not deny.

The next day my father was different. He was filled with the Holy Spirit and spoke the Word of God with boldness to many whom he would not have approached previously. Men like those that bench-pressed things twice their weight in the gym were now fair game to hear about the lifechanging name of Jesus Christ. No longer concerned after the power my father had experienced, his words now held the attention of even the hardest of inmates, many of whom would respond to the gospel over time.

God's presence also became evident through the many volunteers, chaplains, and other inmates who encouraged and discipled my father wherever he went.

At the time, the Montco Prison in Norristown, Pennsylvania, was an old dungeon-like building that resembled a medieval castle. My father spent a memorable two months there in 1986—memorable not because of the dark surroundings but because of the light brought in by the chaplain and volunteers. One volunteer my father met there had been serving and ministering to the inmates at the Norristown jail for 60 years. At 84-years old, he was a character one could not easily forget. When he sang during chapel services and Bible studies, it was clear that he was putting his whole heart into it, and he encouraged others to do so as well.

Popular in those days were songs with lyrics like, "I've got the joy, joy, joy, joy down in my heart." While standing beside him one day, he asked my father, "Do you believe what you are singing?"

"I think so," my father replied.

"Then notify your face."

One of his quotes is something that would become fixed into my father's memory. "Son, if Christianity is anything at all, it's everything."

It was these kinds of ministers and volunteers that God used time after time everywhere my father went.

Many of the circumstances taught my father the Word of God in ways that could not be forgotten. One day, an inmate was attacked and shanked in the throat just outside his cell. As the man lay bleeding, others moved in to steal the victim's shoes and search his pockets. In this particular case, it was Psalm 91 that gave my father comfort.

A thousand may fall at your side, ten thousand at your right hand, but it will not come near you. You will only look with your eyes and see the punishment of the wicked."

Psalms 91:7–8

My father had the entire chapter committed to memory within three days. It actually took longer to get someone to remove the bloodstains from the catwalk outside his cell.

It was those kinds of experiences that firmly planted God's Word in his heart as well as his mind.

Graterford State Prison was another one of those dark places. During his short six-month stay there, my father learned a thing or two about the power of God and worship during a night spent locked up with a devout Satanist named Billy. In for beating up his psychologist, this devil-worshipping roommate was also known for wanting to kill his parents. At one point during the night, Billy started chanting from the top bunk something about bringing curses upon my father, blah, blah, blah. Seriously, spiritual warfare and worship are powerful things, and fortunately my father had learned a thing or two about them by this point. Not knowing what to do exactly, my father just started singing every Christian song and hymn he knew with all his heart. He did not know how long this had been going on, but eventually he stopped to see the man kneeling over the toilet, vomiting violently.

He would later tell my father that he had never been so sick in his life and did not even have the strength to lift his arms to bang on the bed and ask him to stop worshipping. He knew that the singing was causing the severe illness. Needless to say, the chanting did not resume but was replaced with a long string of questions. Billy would later start coming to church with my father and other believers at Graterford and eventually changed his mind about wanting to kill his parents.

It was these kinds of experiences that served as reminders of God's faithfulness and power, even in the darkest of places.

My father also spent some time at Dauphin County Prison in Harrisburg, Pennsylvania. As he faced another trial and considered the consequences of his former lifestyle, the words to this poem flowed seamlessly from a contrite heart:

Altered Minds – Altered Lives
by Allen Emerson

Have a drink or smoke you say, it's alright, it's been rough today.
Don't get me wrong, it's fun at first. But that's the trick, it's Satan's thirst.

So, in alcohol, immerse your brain, take some drugs, just for the pain.
Forget the woes of days gone by, that's what you think, so let's get high.

Now Satan has you by the heart, just where he wanted from the start.
Beware, beware, it's just begun, so many ways he'll show you fun.

You defend the habit by telling lies, the guilt you feel, it's no surprise.
The party friends think you're a winner. The family waits, it's only dinner.

The Hearts of the Fathers

Where did that extra fifty go, oh, that's right
you bought some blow.
The phone and lights will have to wait, you'll
pay'em up when you get straight.

The aches and pains that you've endured, the
dent in the car, well, it's insured.
Are you deaf and dumb, cannot you see? You're
really on a killing spree.

You've killed the love the children had, the
booze, the drugs, it's really sad.
To say the least about the spouse, the love is
gone, 'long with the house.

The spouse, the kids you say you love, they
plead for help from up above.
You'll never see, you think it's right, poor
loving ones, they lost the fight.

All alone in an empty bar, will you make it to
your dented car?
The coke, the smoke, that social drink, it'll
never let you stop and think.

A line of crank, you're on your way, you missed
the light, no time to pray.
The life you had, and now it's gone. Four
others too, at the crack of dawn.

Many altered lives because of an altered mind, in heaven this person, no one will find. All because a lack of faith… All because a lack of faith.

God would use the remainder of my father's prison sentence as a time of intense discipleship, and as he grew in faith, God continued to use him in powerful ways. God was transforming a desperate, bold, creative, radically lost person into someone useful to advance His kingdom and reach other desperate, bold, creative, and radically lost people.

Favorable sentencing and a bit of confusion among the various counties in Pennsylvania had my father released in just over four years. It is easy to look back now to see that God had better things in mind, and the 76 years my father had once faced were not part of God's plan.

43

Not long after his release, my father's calling into prison ministry was confirmed through a series of divine meetings after he connected with a local pastor. His return to New England meant a new life, and his pursuit of new relationships quickly brought new opportunities.

He was invited to attend a Gideon's pastors appreciation luncheon and was introduced to the guest speaker. The topic: Prison Ministry in Vermont—the state my father had lived in for many years.

Upon hearing my father's story, the speaker quickly replied, "There's a meeting you need to go to at 6 o'clock on Sunday."

At that point, my father had no intention of going back into prisons. In fact, he never wanted to see the inside of a prison again.

Confirmation came when my father picked up a hitchhiker along the highway later that week. When he started sharing the gospel with the man, who was already a believer, the hitchhiker responded with the very same words spoken earlier in the week: "There's a meeting you need to go to at 6 o'clock on Sunday."

That meeting would be the start of a 30-year prison ministry career.

The Hearts of the Fathers

Chapter 6

IN THE CROWD

I had joined the Navy right out of high school, got married a year later, and our daughter was born a year after that. My duty stations mainly involved ships that spent a lot of time at sea, with homeports in Norfolk and Charleston. This was difficult for a young marriage, and we were not prepared for the time apart. For that matter, it seemed we were not prepared for the time together either, and unresolved issues were piling up. Separation was a common occurrence, and it was clear that my solutions for dealing with our relationship issues were not working. Heartbreak was also a common occurrence, and the things I was putting my hope in were failing me at an increasing rate.

As lost and let down as I was with my father, I could not help but see a change in him through the things he wrote about and the things he said both while in prison and after his release. These had manifested themselves in peace and joy, and I started to wonder where they were coming from. Deep inside, I was taking notes: *Dad has access to something I don't.* That was about the extent of my understanding at the time. I can specifically remember thinking, *Dad's got religion. Good for him.*

During one particularly painful point, I found myself desperate enough to pick up the phone and call my father. Once again separated from my wife, things were quickly unraveling, and the future looked bleak for our relationship. This was the kind of desperation that causes one to put aside any bitterness or resentment toward another who might be in a position to help. In our previous conversations and letters, my father always referred to the Bible as a resource that had answers for life. I had noticed enough of a difference in my father to see this truth and knew he had access to the kind of power I needed. It was becoming abundantly clear that I did not possess the answers and had come to the end of myself. Simultaneously, the draw I felt toward the call of God on my life was irresistible.

I remember being in a barracks room with another individual in the rack above me. I had gotten my hands on a Bible. Beyond knowing the stories covered in Catholic Sunday school and what little I remembered from summer Bible camps, I had never given this book the opportunity to be relevant in my life. You have to read it after all.

It was the kind of phone call where one party calls the other party in tears.

I told my father what was happening, and through some very painful sobs, my plea was simple: "I have a Bible. What page number do I turn to?"

I did not care about any unresolved issues or the other guy in the room. All I knew was that if this God my dad kept talking about was real, I needed his help. Filled with compassion, my father gave me some Bible passages to read. For the first time, we talked about things that had real substance, things that mattered, things with eternal value.

The relief was real but lasted only a short time. The problem was that I continued trying to fix things on my own, and inevitably, they got worse. A six-month cruise overseas for Operation Desert Shield was next on the agenda, and my ship pulled out on New Year's Eve. Things at home with my wife and daughter had been patched up for the time being but quickly eroded once again after I left.

Just as our operation escalated into the Gulf War, I found myself at the darkest time of my life as I returned to a severely fractured marriage, a broken car, little money, and great uncertainty in the midst of what was supposed to be a homecoming celebration. Our battle group pulled into Charleston Harbor with great fanfare. As others were reunited all around me full of joy, the reality of my situation left me with nothing but emptiness and despair.

Little did I know an important visitor was being escorted from the quarterdeck to where I was on the ship. I got word someone was looking for me just as the door opened to my workspace. I stood in complete disbelief as I recognized my father. He had driven over a thousand miles to be there when my ship arrived.

But it was not his surprise appearance that made the reunions around us pale in comparison. This was not a six-month-absence kind of meeting. This was a reunion-of-a-lifetime, generation-restored kind of meeting.

When I needed him the most, my father showed up. He was in the crowd this time, providing support and resources when I really needed them. As it turned out, I did not really need him all those other times. It would have been nice, but God had been preparing both him and me for this exact moment in time. It was clear that our time together during this period had a divine purpose, much like the orchestrated events my father had experienced in prison.

However, there was still a battle to be won. The draw of the Spirit of God on my broken heart was inescapable. My father came to live with me in South Carolina, and for a while, it was just the two of us. I recall a revival campaign many of the local churches were having that summer. "Here's Hope: Jesus Cares for You" was the unified theme I found myself surrounded by at that critical time.

I remember almost nightly visits to any one of the many congregations that seemed to be located on every street corner. Big churches, small churches, loud music, soft music, dancing, no dancing, you name it. My frame of mind could be summarized by one interaction I had early on with an evangelical pastor.

His question to me was simple: "If you were to die today and stand before God and he were to ask you, 'Why should I let you into my heaven?', what would you say?"

Apparently, the best I could come up with after spending many years in the Catholic Church was, "Because I'm a good person."

This was so deeply embedded into my thinking that it would take years to understand the fundamental issue keeping me from a kind of faith that was not focused on me and my performance. My hope in myself was not working out very well, and I was blinded to the fact that there was a better option.

It was during one such revival night at First Baptist Church of Goose Creek that I recall having a white-knuckle experience that served as the tipping point. I have long since forgotten the preacher's name, but his message finally unlocked a truth I had been missing. So many seeds had been planted by others, and now this unknown minister was there to reap the harvest. With an unyielding grip on the pew in front of me, the altar call had an impact like no other. That better option had been laid out in such a way that all my excuses and pride were exposed, leaving me at the end of myself. For the first time, I came to realize the depth of my depravity and my striving to be a good person was not going to be adequate in the sight of God.

My heart walked down the aisle that night, and I went home, where I fell, broken, on my face. I remember telling God that if he could do something with this mess of a person, then he could have it all. I would serve him. That night I laid all my heartache, brokenness, and sin at the foot of the cross, where I found forgiveness and wholeness through Jesus Christ.

My answer to that very important question about how I was going to get into heaven had changed. My faith was now in someone else's performance. The one who paid the penalty for my sin now stood in my place so that I could have access to the Father. I finally came to understand the profound and exclusive claim made by Jesus in John 14:6.

Jesus said to him, "I am the way, and the truth, and the life. No one comes to the Father except through me."

I also came to understand that if I was accepted, this was an all-inclusive invitation for others.

Another one of the scriptures I remembered from that unknown preacher required action on my part.

Bear with one another and, if anyone has a complaint against another, forgive each other; just as the Lord has forgiven you, so you also must forgive.

Colossians 3:13

Now that I understood why I needed God's forgiveness, I was compelled to pursue forgiveness for, and from, others. The weight removed that night made me want to run to forgive anyone with whom I held a grudge.

Immediately, I drove to the house where my wife and daughter were staying. It was time to clear the air as well as my conscience. I asked my wife forgiveness for everything I could think of and anything I could not. Things had become complicated, and this was helpful in allowing me to move forward.

For once, I could see a way forward and envision a future that had promise and hope.

Chapter 7

REVEREND NIGHTCLUB

With a much different outlook, I immersed myself in things that supported my new life in Christ. I remember going to a small group for those divorced and separated at just 22 years old. It was a bit awkward given the average age of the other attendees who were easily in their 40's. Not a bad place to be actually, surrounded by those with a whole lot more life—and hurt—behind them. I was welcomed with open arms and godly counsel. My father had gone back home, and one blended family in particular was instrumental in helping me navigate what needed to happen next.

Back on the ship, the contrast in my lifestyle did not go unnoticed by others. On earlier deployments, I could be found in the clubs of the Mediterranean ports we visited, often stumbling down the pier after a night of things that sailors do while overseas.

With those days behind me, I could now be found playing guitar in the church services on the ship. I can see how that change would be confusing, and one large African-American shipmate took particular interest.

I worked at the top of the ship with all the electronics, and he would see me from just about any other part of the ship and yell, "Hey, Reverend Nightclub!"

I thought it was persecution at the time, but now I just think it is funny. I eventually became a Protestant lay leader, helping Navy chaplains implement services and Bible studies.

Visits to foreign ports now included much different activities. We regularly connected with Christian missionaries who loved the company of anyone from back home in the States. We would take time to join them on the mission field, where we visited orphanages or participated in their church services. These were exciting times of growth and fruitful relationships, some of which I still have today.

Once back in the States, I eventually moved back to Virginia and, soon after, divorced. Being single and Christian was a fresh new world, however I felt the divorce label set me apart, a reminder of the old self.

I attended a large church in Norfolk, which I remembered noticing from the highway years before under very different circumstances. I visited another divorced and separated group briefly but instead joined a Sunday school class for singles, where I tried to blend in.

Attending a luncheon one day, I was standing in line among singles of the opposite sex when an older gentleman loudly proclaimed, "Hey, don't you go to that divorced and separated group?"

Not helpful, I thought.

It was here that I would meet many people who helped me grow in my faith, and in 1992 I found new love and got engaged. My second marriage meant another wedding, and this time I could think of no better person to be my best man than my father. He had just remarried as well, but I had missed the ceremony because of a deployment.

I spent a number of weeks in New Hampshire after getting out of the military. The opportunity to work with my dad in his flooring business meant enjoying time together mentoring and sharing. It was there that I could see firsthand how my father's testimony was impacting people in exciting ways. For those on the inside, it meant hope and encouragement, with many responding to the gospel. For those on the outside, his before-and-after transformation was tangible among those who knew him.

The Hearts of the Fathers

Chapter 8

THE PHONE BOOK

As the restoration stories started to accumulate, there was a critical one still outstanding. My grandfather remained a mystery, and we did not know how or if my father's prayer from that lonely prison cell in 1984 would be answered. Who would bring the gospel to my grandfather if he was still alive? How would he know that my father had forgiven him?

In 2003, my father traveled to a ministry conference in Florida on behalf of his church. A door had opened for him to go with all expenses paid all the way from where he lived in New England.

The conference lasted a few days and ended on a Friday night. In the hotel room that Friday, he had packed his bags and was preparing to return home the next day. After calling his wife to say good night, he sat on the edge of the bed and flipped open the phonebook on the nightstand.

And there it was. Hidden within the pages of that Crystal River, Florida, phonebook was his name:

Allen M. Emerson

My father remembers thinking, *I wonder if that's my old man.*

He wrote down the number and decided he would call the next day.

In the morning, he left the hotel not knowing exactly where my grandfather lived and drove into town to find a phonebooth. He called the number, and a man answered.

My father could think of only one way to start the conversation. "Sir, did you have a son born in 1948?"

Without hesitation, my grandfather's reply was direct and simple. "Yes, I did."

My father explained who he was and that he was in town, and they agreed to meet. Forty years and a thousand miles apart, they were about to come face to face.

My father was not familiar with the area, so he asked for directions. Looking around, he realized the phonebooth where he stood was just two blocks from my grandfather's house.

Driving the short distance, he turned a corner to see my grandfather waving to him from his yard. Needless to say, my father's travel plans had just changed. For the next week, the two would spend the time catching up and getting to know each other. Reaching this man with the gospel was now possible, and the time they spent together was precious. Their relationship was being restored, and the ground was being prepared for seeds to be planted.

Thinking back on that period of time, I remember a tremendous outpouring of grace as we realized what this meant for our family. God was perfecting that which concerned my father. His prayer for God to send someone was being answered in a way that we could never have imagined. For weeks, I wept in church after my father called with the news of their reunion.

Allen Jr. and Allen Sr. reunited in Florida

But it was not until a year later that I was able to go with my father to that obscure yet miraculous hotel in Florida. We drove down together for my father's birthday, and I was looking forward to meeting my grandfather for the first time. That man my father had prayed for, the sailor I had read about in that colorful service record, the one with so many miles behind him, was now frail and kind. The resemblance to my father was remarkable. His health was not great, but our time together will always be treasured. We visited with him and traveled to his favorite restaurant.

The only picture of the three of us was taken by our
waitress as we shared grouper sandwiches.

For the next nine years, my father and grandfather would call and visit each other often. But the day came when the phone would ring with dire news.

"Your father is not doing very well. He's been admitted to the hospital."

This would be my father's final visit to see him.

As my grandfather lay on his deathbed, my father read the Bible to him. The same book that had touched and changed our hearts was now ministering to my grandfather. He was responsive, but the end of his life was near. The peace and presence of God filled the room as my father shared the words of Jesus in John 14:1.

Do not let your hearts be troubled; believe in God, believe also in me.

As he breathed his last, it was clear by the countenance on his face that my grandfather had come to know this God we too had experienced.

Again, God answered my father's prayer to send someone who would share the gospel with those whom he was concerned. Instead of using other people, God used my father to not only directly reach his "household" but many others as well. God was truly showing him "great and mighty things, which you do not know." (Jeremiah 33:3)

Never could we have imagined the remarkable ways that God would orchestrate circumstances to bring hope to so many through his testimony both inside and outside of prison.

Chapter 9

A BETTER IDEA

The irony found in those newspaper articles from 1984 becomes greater every year. We see now that God can take a checkered past and turn it on its head for His use. The Bible is full of stories of where the devil had evil and destruction in mind yet God redeemed a situation not only for good but restored it on a scale never imagined. The details are never overlooked by God, and sometimes they make the most interesting part of the stories.

For example, my father's crimes had spawned copycats trying to follow in his footsteps and reproduce his "success." Years later, we see his testimony reaching thousands now wanting to follow him to the cross of Jesus Christ. An altogether different kind of success, the impact this story will have on those lives will echo throughout eternity.

When my father's fake bomb threats were emptying rooms all over town, God saw all the rooms that this testimony would fill up with those in need of hearing the gospel. The things my father went through equipped him for a specific purpose to reach many that others cannot. God transformed a desperate, bold, creative, radically lost person into someone useful to advance His kingdom and reach desperate, bold, creative, and radically lost people.

Some of my greatest memories include the times my father and I would go into prisons and share this story. Together with the ministry team from his church, we were regularly surrounded by bleachers filled with inmates who were struggling with bitterness and unforgiveness. Many had children and families they were concerned about, and this stirred many to action. We would share this story and invite them to stand beside us and make a commitment to follow Jesus and serve God. So many would leave their seats that we had to split them up into smaller groups to pray with them.

I had wanted to cut down my family tree, but God had a better idea. His redemption of our hopeless condition has now brought inspiration and hope to many others. He can do the same for you. Impossible situations are his specialty. I would invite you to engage with him today and make the decision to serve God with all your heart.

The Hearts of the Fathers

Chapter 10

THE SPIRIT OF ADOPTION

For all who are led by the Spirit of God are children of God. For you did not receive a spirit of slavery to fall back into fear, but you have received a spirit of adoption. When we cry, "Abba! Father!"
Romans 8:14–15

When we understand the heart of God toward us, we can have the confidence to approach him as children that have been adopted by a loving Father. Through this, we can see how God wants us to treat others who may be fatherless as well. As we receive it, this spirit of adoption is something that overflows in us and is designed to impact others.

In the late '90s, my father and his wife, Doreen, began fostering children in their home right alongside my two stepsisters. Some stayed for short periods of time as the needs arose within the foster care system and some for longer stays. For the next two decades, there was rarely a time when they did not have some connection to an orphan or a child in the system. Every child God brought their way heard about and experienced His love, often when they needed it most.

In 2008 my father and Doreen were introduced to a pair of five-year-old twin boys named David and Phillip. Shy and a little withdrawn, the boys had not experienced a stable home life up to that point. Like others in the foster care system, they had many challenges to overcome, but over time, they opened their hearts to this new family. At age 10 they came to live with my father and Doreen permanently as the adoption process was complete.

Now well over six feet tall each, my new adopted brothers, David (left) and Phillip (right), tower over our dad.

Around the same time my brothers came into the picture, the family continued to expand when my stepsister Heather adopted a very special little boy named Jorgy. Born with multiple conditions related to prenatal substance abuse, Jorgy is full of life and has an incredible sense of humor. His special needs rarely hold him back from filling the home with joy as he continues to grow in health and faith.

Jorgy at age 9

Truly, God sets the lonely in families (Psalm 68:6) and calls us out of fear into a spirit of adoption and the love he has for us. Our response to that adoption as sons and daughters will be seen in how we embrace others who are in need.

Chapter 11

THE BEAT GOES ON

*Your faithfulness endures to all generations;
you have established the earth, and it stands
fast.*
Psalm 119:90

The Bible is filled with God's promises of faithfulness but also our responsibility to declare his works and steadfast love to the next generation. With so many stories of restoration, we thought we would share just a couple from others in our family tree.

One such story comes from my cousin Mark Lacroix. He tells his story in his own words:

"I am fond of telling folks that I am a product of prison ministry. I love the raised eyebrows and odd looks I get because they know I am a public school teacher, and they wonder how that works. But it is true. No, I never served time, but my Uncle Al did. It was my Uncle Al and my cousin BJ who invited me to the tent revival in Claremont, NH, in 1994 where I accepted Jesus as my Lord and Savior. I almost didn't accept the invite to join them that night. In fact, I was back in my car and headed to work my night job as a bartender when I felt a prompting to go back into my grandmother's house, where I had been visiting with BJ. I told him if I had to endure a tent revival for a couple of hours to get to see him and my Uncle Al, then it would be worth it because I did not get to see them that often. The evening of that revival, the course of my life changed. My Uncle Al, a convicted felon turned evangelist, had led my cousin BJ Emerson to Christ. In turn, BJ invited me to the revival, where I realized just how lost I was and found the Lord. Therefore, in a roundabout way, I am a product of prison ministry."

Despite being caught in the middle at times, my daughter has her own amazing story of grace that shows just how concerned God is about the next generation.

She took Emerson as her first name when she got married. In the words of Emerson Fuller:

"As my father mentioned, he and my mother divorced when I was too young to remember. I spent my childhood only seeing him on the rare occasion when he could travel several states away for a short weekend visit or when he had the ability to take me along on vacations to see my extended family. Even though my mother remarried within a year and I grew up with a stepfather, my dad's absence was deeply felt. Growing up, I envied my friends who lived in the same town as their father, and some of them even lived in the same house. Often I would talk about finally getting to see my dad for my birthday or Christmas, and the people we went to church with would get really confused until I explained that the man who was the head of our household was not my biological father. My rebellious spirit clung to the opportunity to reject the authority figure that God had placed in my life while at the same time my young heart reeled every time my dad left from his short visits. That is, until I moved in with him when I was almost sixteen. But those formative years had a deep impact on me. Even though I grew up going to church, I felt rejected. I felt like an afterthought. I felt like I was an outsider and that I only served as a reminder of my parents' brief marriage. You could say I had some 'daddy issues.'

"However, when I came to live with my dad later on, it was a completely different feeling. We attended a church where God drew me in: the youth group fueled my desire to please and connect with others who truly lived for Christ. Honestly, one of the best things my father ever did for me was introduce me to that church. That and finally living under the same roof with my father brought me to a point in my life where I lived in tune with the Holy Spirit and sought out God's truth. God planted desires in my heart for a future that would be different from my family tree—filled with children and a husband who loved God, and me, more than he loved himself.

"When difficulties and heartache occurred shortly after though, the enemy's hold on my mind, and the years I spent feeling rejected, forgotten, and lost, came back with a vengeance. I sought approval from any source I could find, and I numbed the voice of the Holy Spirit when I did so in a way that I knew was against God's will for me. I rebelled, angry at God and lonely in a way that only children that have experienced fatherlessness know.

"In February of 2012 I found myself in the bathroom at my workplace looking down at two little blue lines that landed me in the deepest pit of fear I had ever known. Not only was I pregnant but I wasn't even in a relationship. My little girl didn't even have a chance at knowing her father because I didn't even know who he was. (I later found out that he was a convicted felon with a history of abuse and assault.) My heart broke in that bathroom. I thought I had experienced pain before, but I knew at that point in my life that something had to change. This cycle had to break. I had finally hit rock bottom, and I knew that only one thing could get me back on my feet again: God. He was the only one who could save me and my daughter from the pain and heartbreak I went through.

"I would like to be able to say that I lived life perfectly over the next five years, according to what God's Word tells single mothers, but I didn't. However, when my sins came back to bite me, this time I wasn't surprised. I repented and moved on. During this time, God showed up in my life in so many ways. Only by his grace was I able to provide for my daughter on my own, which not all young single mothers are able to do. We had our own apartment, and I relied very little on monetary help from either of my parents. I attended a church that was supportive and authentic. Then, in the fall of 2016, when I was working two jobs and taking five classes while my daughter was in daycare seventy hours a week, I met my future husband and the man who would adopt my daughter as his own. He fell in love with me because of my tenacity and drive—things I would not have developed had I not been through all that I had. His heart broke for me and my daughter when he heard my story, and he desired to walk alongside me in life, caring for me in a way that I had never experienced.

"Finally, God had fulfilled the dreams and desires he had put in my heart when I was only sixteen. There are a million ways in which I could have gotten even more lost, but God protected me from each one of them and guided me to the abundantly loving life I now live. In spite of the statistics and in spite of the stigmas, God took my story and used me to show how awesomely powerful he truly is. My daughter may not ever know her biological father, but she knows who her Heavenly Father is. In part, that's due to the influence of my father and her adoptive father. She will know my story and my father's and grandfather's stories. She will know God's faithfulness and his love. She and my other children will know that regardless of their experience with their earthly father, God is the ultimate daddy. He is Abba Father, and only he will provide all of our greatest needs."

Adopted into the Emerson family at an early age, Phillip Emerson shares his perspective:

"When I came to the Emerson family from the orphanage at age five, I was a broken kid from a broken family.

"It was my dad who helped me understand I'm made in the image of God and what it means to be a follower of Jesus. I feel like my life would have been wasted and I'd still be in an orphanage, maybe caught up in drugs or worse.

"I remember my dad reading a verse in the Bible that says the devil is here to steal, kill, and destroy. I understand now that I have the choice of listening to the devil or praying to God when I am in trouble or being attacked.

"When I was in a rough spot and in the hospital, my dad came and continuously prayed for me, reading the Bible every night. He's been there for me the most, and I thank him for bringing me up in a Christian home. I know I can overcome with God our Father and my savior Jesus Christ.

"People in this world always want to be famous but not me. I wish I was like my dad. He may not be famous to the world, but he sure is famous to God and to me."

The Hearts of the Fathers

For Those Incarcerated

If you are reading this from prison, I have not been where you are. But I have been where your children are. While you may not be able to be with them physically, know that your prayers are heard by a loving Heavenly Father, and he can do miracles when we put our faith in him to do what we cannot. His concern for you goes beyond what you can imagine. Do not be surprised if he chooses you to impact your family and others right where you are despite your circumstances.

If you are still putting your faith in yourself, look to Jesus and know that forgiveness is available to you through his sacrifice on the cross. Put your trust in the one who can forgive and restore.

My father's prayers from prison changed the course of history for our family and have impacted generations. Your prayers can do the same.

Reach out to God today with this simple prayer:

Heavenly Father, I come to you admitting that my sin has separated us. I confess with my mouth and believe with my heart that your Son Jesus died for me and rose again. I turn from my sins and ask for your forgiveness through Jesus for eternal life. I choose to follow him all my days. Thank you for loving me.
In Jesus' name,
Amen

Questions for Discussion

Regardless of where you are in your faith, consider and share the questions below with others who will help you grow toward what God has for you.

Chapter 1
Think about a time when you were hopeless. What kept you from seeing that God had something better in mind for you?

Chapter 2
What kind of generational issues are you struggling with?
What got handed down to you that still needs to be addressed?

Chapter 3
What layers of bitterness are you holding on to?
How is this keeping you from growing in your faith?

Chapter 4
Who are the people in your life that God is using to draw you closer to him?
Who are the people you are concerned about that need Jesus?

Chapter 5
How has God helped you grow in your faith through trials?
In what ways has he used you to reach others?

Chapter 6
In what ways have you found the Bible provides you with answers for life?
What were your questions?

Chapter 7
What does your before-and-after story look like?
What would your "Reverend Nightclub" name be?

Chapter 8
What miraculous reunion are you hoping for?
How has God demonstrated his faithfulness
toward you?

Chapter 9
In what ways has the devil tried to destroy
your life?
How has God turned that around for your
good?

Chapter 10
Have you understood and received the
adoption that God offers you as a son or
daughter?

Chapter 11
How will you declare God's works and
steadfast love to the next generation?

The Hearts of the Fathers

Share the Hope

We encourage you to share this book with others and hope you can write to let us know how this story has impacted you.

The Hearts of the Fathers
Attn: BJ Emerson
P.O. Box 30322
Greenville, NC 27833

Others can visit our Facebook page to request a copy:

Facebook.com/TheHeartsOfTheFathersBook